Breaking Functional Dysfunction

By Jessica Amber James, MSW

Social Worker/ Certified Life Coach

Breaking Dysfunctional Behaviors and Relationships,
and Creating a Purpose Driven Life in 21 Days

Books Speak For You books may be ordered through booksellers or by contacting:
Publisher @Booksspeakforyou.com
1-800-757-0598
The views expressed in this work are solely those of the Author, Jessica Amber James.

Any illustration provided by iStock and such images are being used for illustrative purposes.
Certain stock imagery © iStock.
ISBN: 978-1-64050-299-4
Printed in the United States of America

Author Biography

Jessica A. James is a New Jersey Native who has always had an interest in serving her community. With a Life Coaching Certification, a Bachelor's Degree from Morgan State University in Sociology, and a Master's Degree from Southern University at New Orleans in Social Work; Jessica is driven by her love of people. She's battled through depression, low self-esteem, and toxic relationships. Through salvation Jessica has turned her life around, and devotes her time to helping individuals reach their optimum potential. She believes every person has the innate ability to change, and uses proven knowledge and evidence-based practices to enhance people's lives. Through her own experiences Jessica advocates for mental health stability, and a fulfilling life.

Acknowledgement

To God You're a Real One for loving me unconditionally, My Support Team, and Thank you to the many people who walked away

Preface

Breaking Functional Dysfunction is a 21-Day Course started by Certified Life Coach/ Social Worker Jessica A. James. As she viewed the parallel between dysfunctional behaviors and high functional individuals, she realized the dire need for mental health. If you are battling with depression, low self-esteem, or toxic relationships this book is for you. The course is designed to begin with childhood trauma and help you unpack adverse experiences to lead a fulfilling and happy life. This book is based on evidence-based practice, and uses proven principles that truly work. This book doubles as a reading and workbook. Each day you read the passage and write directly in the book like a journal. If you're ready to be free from dysfunctional behaviors, and repeating toxic relationships give this book a try.

Chapter 1 Childhood

This workbook will change the course of your life. It will unlock secrets to success, stopping bad habits, and help you gain clarity in your everyday life. High functioning dysfunctional people like myself have extreme success and terrible failures at the same time. We can appear successful on our exterior, and silently crumble on the inside. High functioning dysfunction affects people from all walks of life. Dysfunction is passed down generationally, and we have the options to adapt and heal or continue a legacy of dysfunction. My childhood like most families was filled with poverty, acute trauma, and rough patches. The problem did not stem from having a hard childhood, the problem stemmed from not learning how to heal from it. I've always marveled at other people's stories how they came from nothing, and turned it around became successful and can have a dedicated group of friends and marriage. My story was certainly not the worse, and yet I found myself consistently bound by things I should've left in my childhood. Kaiser Permanente and the Centers for Disease Control and Prevention conducted a study on Adverse Childhood Experiences. Adverse Childhood Experiences (ACE) are stressful or traumatic events that can have negative, lasting effects on health and well-being. Although my childhood wasn't lavish, I also didn't believe it was the worse, so I assumed I had no (ACEs). Wrong. It wasn't until I reached a breaking point of serious depression that I began diving into my childhood to find a connection. This first exercise requires complete honesty and vulnerability. Flash back to your childhood to pour out the complete truth, and not the watered-down version you've told yourself to feel better about yourself. Do not play victim and do not down play life events, as I will ask you to expose yourself in our workbook. No one likes to bring up past feelings and emotions, but I promise by the end of the 21 days it will all be connected.

Chapter 1 Activity

Below are fill in the blank exercises about 10 types of childhood trauma. In a few words jot down your memories if any of these pertain to you.

Physical Abuse

_____

_____

_____

Sexual Abuse

_____

_____

Emotional Abuse

_____

_____

Physical Neglect

_____

_____

Emotional Neglect

_____

Violence in the Home

_____

_____

Household Substance Abuse

_____

_____

Household Mental Illness

_____

_____

Parental Separation, Divorce, Incarceration, or Absentee

_____

_____

Bullying

As you're probably digging into your past with your deepest secrets exposed, I want you to reflect on this verse from the Bible found in Jeremiah 29:11 "For I know the plans I have for you, declares the Lord, plans to prosper you and not to harm you, plans to give you a hope and a future." Today's assignment wasn't to bring up hurtful emotions, but to make you completely vulnerable to God. He knows everything that has happened to you, and I can already hear you now; then God shouldn't have let me go through that!! I'm here to offer another perspective. What if everything was perfect in your life? Life would be bland

and very routine. You would've never learned to walk if you didn't fall. Sometimes our best lessons come from our past, what we did and didn't get, who hurt us, who left, and how we messed up. Perhaps life isn't about reaching a perfect destination of happiness with absence of conflict. Perhaps life is about learning to dance in the rain when you've received a storm. Today mediate on acceptance of the past. Not for anyone else's benefit but yours. Look over the list and say a prayer to God helping you to accept the things you cannot change.

Chapter 2 Acceptance of Childhood Trauma

Acceptance is defined as a "willingness to tolerate a difficult or unpleasant situation." In this life, regardless of economic, religious, or ethnic background every single person will have pain in this life time. I do not agree with people who say successful people are successful because they've mastered their pain. There are plenty of successful people on the verge of suicide because of silent depression due to unresolved issues from their childhood. When I made my list of Adverse Childhood Experiences I was astounded by my results. I came from a working-class family had both parents, and I still qualified in every category. There are hidden traumas especially in the minority communities that we don't even consider trauma such as excessive violence at home, alcoholism and smoking weed as a substance abuse, even inappropriate fondling or unwanted sex from a family member or partner. We must get very raw with this acceptance that we have justifiable hurt, unexplained emotional anguish which we pass off as "anger issues" or the worst selective memory. Acceptance is not pushing your emotions to the side, its allowing yourself to feel everything that has happened to you to move on. Acceptance is gaining a tolerance of pain inflicted on you and learning to not repeat it to other people. The easiest part of my list was writing it. Accepting my experiences, and not judging others by it was going to take hard work. For instance, my father was alive, but he was absent most of my childhood. He was busy working, drinking, partying, and cheated on my mother. I didn't believe his actions affected me until I grew old enough to date. For the life of me I couldn't understand why men chase me down, dated me, and left me as soon as I wanted commitment. I cried many tears, because I wanted one man to stay and give me consistency. I unknowingly repeated my hurt from my father in my relationships. I never saw consistency, so when I snagged a man I unknowingly gave him my heart up front and all my mess, because I needed someone to pick up the load of disappointment I had been carrying for so long. I neglected to even care that the man would probably be carrying his own load, and couldn't handle that type of pressure. So, I scared him off and for years I played the blame game, until I made a list and saw the lesson connect.

Chapter 2 Activity

Write a sentence for every Adverse Childhood Experience explaining the lesson it taught you. An example from my life would be Emotional Neglect- My father was alive, but inconsistent when I was growing up. Lesson Sentence- I learned that it wasn't my fault my father was absent from my life. His father was absent from his life, and was mirroring his example. He was also suffering from other physical and emotional traumas himself. I learned true

forgiveness

_____

_____

_____

_____

_____

_____

_____

_____

_____

_____

_____

_____

_____

Chapter 3 All Bark No Bite

At one point or another many of us share the same story of childhood bullying. When we look back at the past we can laugh now, but while we were experiencing being bullied it sure didn't feel funny. In middle school, I had mocha dark skin, hair that would never grow past my shoulders, a horrible underbite, and an unproportioned body that was shaped like a capitol letter P. I was constantly teased, and told I resembled a Grandma; my self-esteem took a total hit. So, I hit the local beauty supply store and brought some weave and makeup and BAM; I was back in action. One day I was jumping double-dutch with my new pony tail at recess thinking I was cute, and a bully came and snatched off my pony tail in front of the entire recess. Talk about embarrassing. Instead of crying in front of everyone, because I wasn't a punk, I proceeded to yoke the kid up by the collar and we almost came to blows. Someone pulled me off him and that's where I learned anger is a second emotion that masks other bottled up emotions. I was embarrassed, shamed, hurt, and mistreated, but expressing anger made me feel in control. Expressing my anger made me feel that no one was going to mess with me again, little did I know that was a piece of the root to a dysfunctional life for me. No one offered me this secret that I'll share with you. The earliest meaning of the word bully in the 1530s meant "sweetheart," applied to either sex, from Dutch word boel meaning "lover" or brother. Perhaps from another perspective your childhood bullies were infatuated with you. Any time you came into the room you became the topic of discussion. In my opinion no one pays attention to something that isn't worth speaking of. Whether they were telling the truth or lies, there was something about you that intimidated the people who talked about you. What if we were taught not to be bothered by our haters, but to empower ourselves that we are worth talking about. Some people talk about us, because it's the truth and we may need to correct ourselves. In other instances, we get put down and belittled for no fault of our own. What if we took our power back from everyone that has had anything negative to say, and turn it into a positive?

Chapter 3 Activity

Write down things you've been bullied about in the past, and write a reverse positive statement. For example, I was bullied because I had an underbite and kids would call me grandma. My positive statement is: Kids called me grandma as an insult, but as the years have gone on I learned I'm a wise beautiful young woman with an old-school soul, and it's a blessing in disguise.

_____

_____

_____

_____

_____

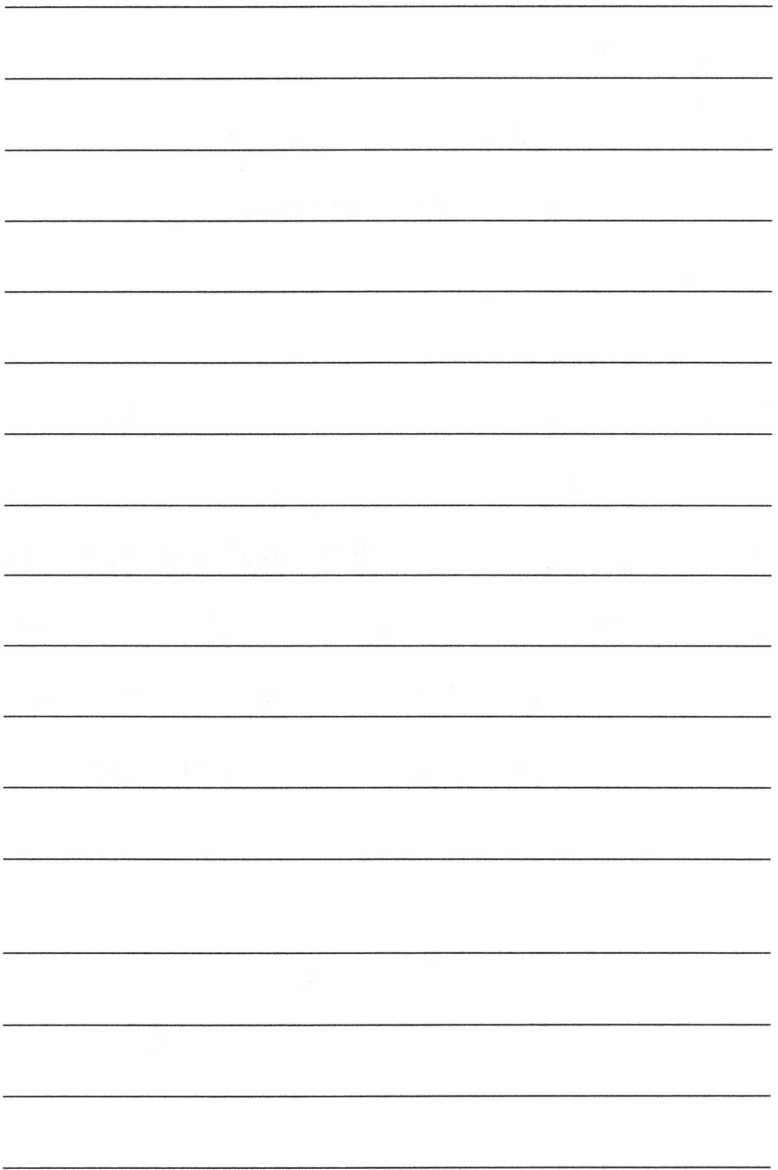

Chapter 4 Keep My Name Out Your Mouth

We all know the phrase sticks and stones may break my bones but words will never hurt me. In my experience, I don't know a person who hasn't experienced pain, hurt, or disappointment from words spoken in this lifetime. It is important as we begin to reflect on our younger selves, to evaluate the words and labels people have spoken over us. There is a direct connection between the words spoken of you, and the roles you've assumed in life. Labeling theory is rooted in the idea of the social construction of reality, which is central to the field of sociology. Labeling theory posits that people come to identify and behave in ways that reflect how others label them. It is most commonly associated with the sociology of crime and deviance, where it is used to point out the social processes of labeling and treating someone as criminally deviant fosters deviant behavior. It is critical to take self-inventory of the labels that your parents, relatives, and peers have placed on you even as a child. Have you ever been labeled negatively as bad, promiscuous, uneducated, poor, etc.? Despite my academic achievements and many accomplishments, I was negatively labeled all the time. I was labeled as poor, weak, indecisive, whorish, sneaky, and many other things. It's not to say that any of these labels were a lie, but perhaps from another perspective I'd began adapting to the labels put on me. I began believing the negative labels about myself. Even if I tried to change my behavior my peers would quickly remind me of my negative label and treat me accordingly. It wasn't until a Student Activities Advisor in my University took a keen interest in me, and dropped subtle hints that I was worth something. I looked at her life. She was well-respected and well-dressed and I wanted that for myself. I began removing the negative labels off myself without the permission of others. I created the change I wanted to see in myself. I began throwing out my tub tops and mini-skirts for fashionable (cheap) business casual dresses on clearance at department stores. I loved the responses from women and men I was receiving on my more appropriate attire. The way I dressed was honestly how I was getting addressed by men and women. Men would look at me and automatically assume I was promiscuous and women would snicker behind my back. It took one loving woman to correct me without judgement to finally realize I could create new labels for myself. I literally became the woman I always wanted to be

Chapter 4 Activity

Describe the negative labels that people have placed on you. Whether they are true or false explain. Then write a new label for yourself. Example I was labeled as promiscuous New Label- I am a Queen full of value, talent, and worthy of love. (Side Note: You can write your new labels on sticky post-its to recite to yourself every day until

you become the person you want to be)

_____

_____

_____

_____

_____

_____

_____

_____

_____

_____

_____

_____

_____

Chapter 5 Respect Your Roots

As we evolve from the reflection of youth we must consider our parents and the role they play in our lives. No one predicts the hardships and storms that life throws at us. No matter how many books or online videos watched, nothing can prepare you to parent your child like only you can. A child is a gift from God specially hand delivered to parents to help guide through this life. Some pregnancies were planned others were not, but the fact remains that God looked at you and saw the world needed one of you too. One of the issues I had with my parents was resentment with my upbringing. I continued to focus on what I didn't receive, and began searching the world for a love I should've received at home. That's not to say that my family didn't love me or wasn't showing me; it was simply negative thoughts telling me to focus on everything wrong in my family, and not on everything that was or could be right. For a family to be "functional" today, there should be a mother, a father, a stable clean home environment, education, access to healthcare, absence of physical, sexual, or emotional violence or neglect, and economic stability. So right there almost all of us have or will fall short in one category. The hurt deepens when we are missing many of these components. We feel isolated like God decided to give us imperfect families while everyone else is living in their perfection. I've come to offer another perspective, what if the life given was in preparation of your success? Many successful people have very harsh childhoods, and they've used it as a driving force to make a better life for themselves. I dare you to research your favorite idol or CEO and dig into their past. Inevitably, you will understand that it's not where you come from, but where you are going. As sign of maturity, I had to learn to stop blaming my parents for what I didn't have, and be grateful for exactly where I am today. It was pointless to be angry about not getting name brand shoes when I understood people walked streets without them, new clothes for every occasion when someone didn't have clothes to attend school, eating my favorite meal when someone didn't eat dinner and their only meal would be at the school lunch. We grieve our parents not understanding the magnitude of the sacrifices made. We then have the nerve to skip school, disrespect them, and not clean the house they provide for us. No matter if you have one parent, both, kinship, or foster parents if your parents mean well, love and support you, do their best by you; you owe it to cherish them. If you've found yourself in a situation where you may not have that support system; I encourage you to pray earnestly to God, and he will allow you to find the right people who can step in for you. There are mentors across the world if you seek you shall find. Remember life is not the clothes we had or the cars we drove, but the positive impact we left on the world.

Chapter 5 Activity

Create a Grateful List of Your life. Take self-inventory of your surroundings you'll be surprised at how blessed you truly are (Example I am grateful for a roof over my head every night)

- I am grateful for
- I am grateful for
- I am grateful for
- I am grateful for
- I am grateful for
- I am grateful for
- I am grateful for
- I am grateful for
- I am grateful for

Part II Self

Chapter 6 It's all in Your Mind

There is virtually no difference between you and your favorite person to look up to. There is no genetic difference between a janitor and a CEO. We all have the same 24 hours in the day, the same human genetic makeup, but there is one difference, our thoughts. You can think yourself into owning a Fortune 500 company or into a dark depression the choice is yours. Look around you, every business you see, every item in your house, every great musical artist began with a thought. A creative thought then formalized into a plan, and success followed. Your thoughts can make you happy or miserable. I had a bad habit of "comparison-driven thinking." I would casually glance at social media throughout the day, and most times feel completely depressed about my own life. I started to see my peers get married, travel more, and live these exciting lives, while I was silently drowning. Most of the time, I was happy for my friends, and their success, but there was a silent knife to my ego, as my life was not seeming successful. The moment something changed for me when a friend made a powerful statement. She asked me "Why do you treat stranger better than yourself?" I was confused, and began a self- evaluation. It was true! I would cheer other people on, constantly check their social media, and praise their good works. I decided right there I was going to become my biggest cheerleader. When I developed negative or jealous thoughts I would counteract those thoughts with something in my life I was grateful for. My mind would wander on negative self-doubting thought all day, and for a while I believed I had to listen, and beat myself up. One day I just stopped, and started writing down all the harming thoughts that came to mind for just one day. The list was overwhelming. How crazy of me to praise other people, and destroy myself. My positive thinking had positive effects on my social life, because newsflash no one wants to be around a person who is constantly depressed, petty, or mean. The way you treat others is a direct reflection of how you treat yourself. What if you treated yourself with understanding and compassion, what if you complimented yourself, what if you have a million-dollar dream inside of you, but you're cheating yourself out of it with your thoughts every day?

Chapter 6 Activity

Today you will listen to your thoughts. We have on average 50,000-70,000 thoughts per day. Some are negative and some are positive. Write down your thoughts throughout the day negative on one side, and positive on the other. You will be able to see the direction your thoughts are driving you in.

Negative Thoughts	Positive Thoughts

Chapter 7 Self Evaluation

As we begin to understand the power of our thoughts, we can understand the power of our actions. We cannot control everything that happens to us, but we can control our responses. Newton's third law of motion states: For every action, there is an equal and opposite reaction. Whether negative or positive I would have to give an equal reaction. One of my biggest obstacles in my life was controlling my reaction to people. I consider myself a quietly sensitive person. That would mean from the outside I appeared confident and strong, but if someone hurt me; I immediately turned to aggression or inward isolation from those people to deal with my problem. It wasn't until someone mentioned to me that no one on this earth had the ability to hurt my feelings if I didn't allow them to. There is a conscious choice in every situation to allow myself to be hurt. For example, I had a friend who I thought was speaking negatively about me behind my back, but wouldn't confront me in person. We ended up at the same dinner function where anyone could tell the energy and vibe was completely off. I was having a war in my mind about how to handle the situation. As the night was winding down I decided I couldn't take the pressure of appearing to ignore the situation. I already addressed the person before about making comments to which everything was denied, but my intuition told me otherwise. I had a decision to make should I lash out and confront the person to make her understand her actions, or was there another way to handle the situation. I decided to remove myself from the situation quietly without hassle. I heard God whisper to me that I was on the right track, and that was extreme growth. That was the first time I felt in control of my emotions. But just like any situation the test is never over; God just graduates you to handle situations on a bigger scale. I ended up celebrating a friend's birthday over the weekend, and that same person was present. I had to make a very crucial decision. I couldn't just leave the weekend gathering and I couldn't approach the person as that was going to completely ruin the weekend for everyone else on the trip. I had to stare my emotions in the face, and control them. The lesson taught me I must never give anyone else my happiness. Even if someone gave me a negative vibe, didn't want to be around me etc. I didn't have to entertain negativity. I'd become content with myself, loving myself, and treating myself with more respect; I could no longer tolerate anyone who didn't do the same. So, I stuck it out, even made conversation, and refused to be a victim to my emotions any longer. The weekend went well without any arguments, fights, or feelings of isolation. You've got to do a self-evaluation of your reaction patterns. People will always talk about you, get on your nerves, or belittle you, you are solely responsible for your response. Choose today how to respond to the world.

Chapter 7 Activity

Create a self-evaluation of how you respond to negativity. Avoidance, isolation, aggression, and violence are among the common negative responses. Write down positive responses you can do from now on,

-
-
-
-
-
-
-
-

Chapter 8 Mental Health

Your mind is your most valuable asset. It gives you the ability to wake up each morning, get your body in motion, and to achieve great things. The difference between the depressed you and the happy you, is your mind. The bible explains the thief comes only to steal and kill and destroy (John 10:10) If your mind is your ticket to happiness and success, the enemy musters up all his strength to attack that place. You must protect your peace, your sanity, and the one mind God gave you. Your mind is so important that almost any other place in the body can fail and be healed, but when a person is brain dead, the body completely shuts down. It is imperative daily to keep watch over your thoughts and the health of your mind. Right before I graduated with my Master's Degree I had a mental breakdown. There was no warning, and no manic episode. I had been silently suffering for months, and keeping myself busy with social activities. When I hit my sheets at nights there was a secret discontentment I had with life. A collection of financial stress, educational stress, work load, dysfunctional relationships, and my mind could take no more. I felt like I wanted to end it all, because my dysfunctional behavior had finally caught up to me, and I felt like an isolated failure. Satan was whispering to me that I wasn't important, no one would ever love me, and that I didn't even have a purpose on this earth. I believed him more and more, but I had a praying momma. She taught me in times of distress to call on the name of Jesus for help. After a small prayer, I immediately got on the phone and wept uncontrollably to my mom, and she began interceding in prayer for me. Instantaneously I felt calm and at peace. She told me if God didn't have a purpose for my life I wouldn't be here. There were over 100 million sperm cells that raced to the egg, and your strongest one survived. Don't quit before God can fully use you, and give the devil exactly what he wants. No one cares about your history until you win in life, so you've got to overcome and win. That day I understood the power of thoughts, and that my mental health mattered. From the outside looking in I appeared happy, beautiful, a girl who had everything she ever wanted or needed. On the inside I was completely torn. I'll never forget a man compared me to a beautiful house. There were many visitors inquiring from the outside, some even prepared to make an offer to come and love me. When the doors of the house opened, the house was in shambles.; no structure, messy places, and dark depression lingered all over the house. The people who came ran fast away just as quickly. It was then I decided to seek professional counseling, and admit to myself my mental health truly mattered.

Chapter 8 Activity

Journal your mental health in its present state. What emotions do you experience on the regular? If you have

more negative emotions than positive, what can you change
to have a happier life?

_____

_____

_____

_____

_____

_____

_____

_____

_____

_____

_____

_____

_____

_____

Chapter 9 Every Good Thing

Society teaches us to be as close to perfection as possible. We are supposed to be in shape, make money, travel, have perfect teeth, perfect credit, good friends, and always be happy. If you happen to fall out of the lines of perfection by making mistakes society is quick to cast you away. It's not that you can't change your imperfect behavior, it just may take you longer than other people. It took me years to understand my mistakes did not disqualify me from receiving every good thing. Humankind looks on the outward appearances while God searches your heart. When I developed a heart after God, and allowed him to create better character in me, my life started improving. However, the people who knew the old me would be first to belittle me, and remind me of my past mistakes. If you aren't careful you can allow other people to convince you that you aren't worthy of every good thing. There is a common myth that one cannot turn a hoe into a housewife. That statement perpetuates dysfunction and failure. There is no sin too big or too small that God can't forgive. From experience, the more I surrendered myself to God the happier and blessed I became. I began telling myself my past mistakes did not determine my future. I had to become better, so I could attract better. When I was insecure and needy of a relationship, I attracted men who would just use me. Instead of waiting for God my dysfunction would attract more dysfunction in my life. I hated being alone watching everyone else have great relationship success even my previous lovers. Many nights I cried, and asked God why couldn't I have the love everyone else had. God answered me and said because you've put the idea of loving a man before me. He said you've cried and worried about a man I've already set aside for you, but you haven't cried or worried about your inconsistent relationship with me. Instead of focusing on becoming the woman and wife I was meant to be I was busy making marriage an idol. I had to ask myself, even if I never got married would I still love and trust God. It was there I vowed to seek first the kingdom of God, and his righteousness, and he will give me everything I need. (Mathew 6:33)

Chapter 9 Activity

If we aren't careful we can disqualify ourselves from good things worrying about our past mistakes. We can turn this around today by claiming every good thing that God has for our life. Begin seeing yourself as the person you ultimately want to be with I deserve statements. Give yourself more credit.

- I deserve
- I deserve
- I deserve
- I deserve
- I deserve
- I deserve

- I deserve

- I deserve

- I deserve

- I deserve

- I deserve

- I deserve

- I deserve

- I deserve

- I deserve

Chapter 10 Self-Love

There's going to come a time when the answers to all your problems stem from self-love. You're going to be tired of hearing it from multiple people. We ultimately want to envision ourselves as self-love ambassadors, but our actions don't always line up with our thoughts. The ultimate lesson in self-love is that I am 100% responsible for my actions, the people I allowed to treat me badly, the weight I've gained, and the dysfunctional thoughts friendships, and partners I've had in my life. Understand this statement; self-love is ugly before it becomes beautiful. You must sit in the guilt and shame of your past mistakes, and forgive yourself. You must address physically or theoretically unaddressed issues from previous friends, relatives, or career choices. You must choose nights where your phone doesn't ring, and you're not invited to outings, because you need to have more positive friends in your circle. Solitude is not punishment, sometimes God needs to talk to you, and you have too much outside noise. You must learn to be alone and lean on God. It means closing the social media app comparing your life to others, and becoming overwhelmingly selfish with yourself. You can literally miss your blessings or opportunities in life watching celebrities have their success. It means posting sticky notes of encouragement, and self-love statements until you believe them. Self-love is very emotional, lonely, and scary at first, and slowly it's the most liberating process you will ever go through. You will be stable in your own life, and begin attracting more positive people to your circle. You will be content in your own skin. You won't have to chase people that do not want to stay in your life. When you focus on reaching your goals the universe will reward you, because you've put out productive energy, which must come back to you. It took me awhile to finally be okay with being single, with having less than 5 close friends, to opt out of happy hours or events I truly didn't want to attend, to love my body as I was working towards my weight loss goals, and to finally choose myself. Choose yourself every day, every moment, and with every thought. Choose to become the person you want to be. Choose those creative thoughts in your head that you belittle. Choose your dreams, because we only have one life to live. Why live your life constantly wanting to be someone different? Be that person today. Dysfunction cannot thrive in an environment full of love. When you love yourself you're more kind to others, you'll be more empathetic and patient, you'll bypass anyone who wants to mistreat you, because you're treating yourself with love, honor, and respect. Dysfunction thrives in bitterness, anger, emotional instability, and stress. Choose today to leave your dysfunctional functioning for a life of clarity through self-love.

Chapter 10 Self Love Activity

List 10 things you like about yourself. It's important to recognize the areas we should work on, but the good will always outlast the bad. Focus on what is right about you.

_____

_____

_____

_____

_____

_____

_____

_____

_____

_____

_____

Part 3 Purpose

Chapter 11 Where do I begin?

Once you've confronted your past, and began to love on yourself the next step is purpose. There have been many books, motivational speakers, and teachers who've taught on purpose. With all the knowledge,available, everyone should have an easy time figuring out their true purpose on earth. I wish that was true, but it isn't. To find your purpose, you must dig deeper than you've ever been before. You must take an assessment of your entire life. The assessment should begin from childhood. What came naturally to you that other people have a hard time with? What were you given awards throughout the course of your life for? When you turn on the television what show could you easily watch all day? What events do you gravitate to other than socially? Your purpose has silently pushed you to it since you were a child. We sometimes get drowned out by our adverse experiences that we will block out purpose for convenience. From my childhood, I've always been a leader. Whether it was forming a new girl group, or starting a step team, I was even preaching to my stuffed animals and was saved by the age of 10. I was labeled a book worm, and even won awards for my not-so-cool hobby. I loved to get lost in books, and wrote in journals all the time. Reading was my favorite past time. I grew older, and began straying away from the right path, not because I didn't love God but I wanted to experiment. My experimentation led me to sex outside of marriage, drunk nights, angry episodes, and much confusion. I believed in my heart God still wanted to use me for something, but I told myself I was disqualified from my calling, because I wasn't worthy of it. The beautiful thing about God is that he doesn't call the qualified, he qualifies the called. God kept interrupting my relationships, my happiness, and even closing career doors, because he was determined to use me.

I kicked and screamed, and even tried to get a "safer" career choice, because I never wanted success God's way. He kept urging me to tell my story, but I was too ashamed. So, I began writing this book a month after graduating with a Master's Degree and completely unemployed. I aced my interviews, had great references, and was overly qualified for the jobs. I hit rock bottom, and that's when God said I hope you've exhausted yourself trying to do it your way. I surrendered with no income, a nonexistent love life, friends coming and going; I decided to write. I found my passion and purpose, and it looked nothing like what I had in mind. You've got to allow God to show you your purpose. It's not what your family wants, what your partner wants, it's what God wants. Outside of your marital status, income level, or education attainment; the question is who are you, and what do you want to be? I don't believe that we don't know our purpose in life. I believe we disqualify ourselves with thoughts of inadequate money, failure, non-risk taking, and comfort level. If I gave you money for the rest of your life, and you had to do something that didn't involve working what would you passionately do that brings fulfillment?

Chapter 11 Activity

Write down your biggest dream. Use your imagination, forget about finances, haters, or anyone else and be selfish for a moment. When you pass away in this life what do you want to be remembered for?

_____

_____

_____

_____

_____

_____

_____

_____

Chapter 12 Protect Your Purpose

This journey of clarity will be exciting and exonerating, yet it will prove to be dangerous. Many times, we want to share our dreams and goals with the people closest to us. We want our friends and family to support our journey. In many cases, genuine support helps us to obtain our goals. In other cases, the lack of support or "secret jealous support" could starve our dreams and goals. The ability to decipher who to surround yourself with can make the difference between success or mediocrity. Some characteristics of positive support systems are people who celebrate you or promote you without being asked, and not expecting anything in return. Positive support systems aren't seeking "discounts" on your merchandise. They are your cheerleaders, positive energy, and people who love you with or without success. Pay attention to those who do not clap for you when you win. Characteristics of negative support systems can be tricky. Everyone may not have negative words to say to you, and these people may in fact appear to support your dreams, but their actions won't line up. They may show up for your achievements, but have underhanded negative things to say about you. They will belittle your dreams to match their reality. Watch the people who can sit in a negative conversation about you, and won't defend you. Many of these people can identify the successful calling on your life, and they will stay close in hopes of reaping the benefits. It is crucially important in the beginning stages of your goal setting to protect it. That requires possible isolation, keeping negative conversations to a minimum, not prematurely telling people or social media, and allowing God to direct your footsteps. It may seem easy, but I've allowed many people to distract and derail me from my course by talking too much. Be careful with friends who always bring you gossip and negativity about other people, as they can run and tell your business to others. As you begin to value yourself and believe in your dreams you'll realize it's more important to do more than you say. It's time to focus on completing the goals, and not convincing everyone that you can. It's your time to be selfish and focused on the purpose God has for your life. God didn't give your purpose to anyone else, so seek guidance and provision from him, he ultimately is the only one who has the answers for you. Protect your energy, protect your mind, and protect your purpose.

Chapter 12 Activity

Identify who your positive support system is. You will become like your 5 closest friends. Evaluate your circle, and identify how you can have a more positive support system.

_____

_____

_____

_____

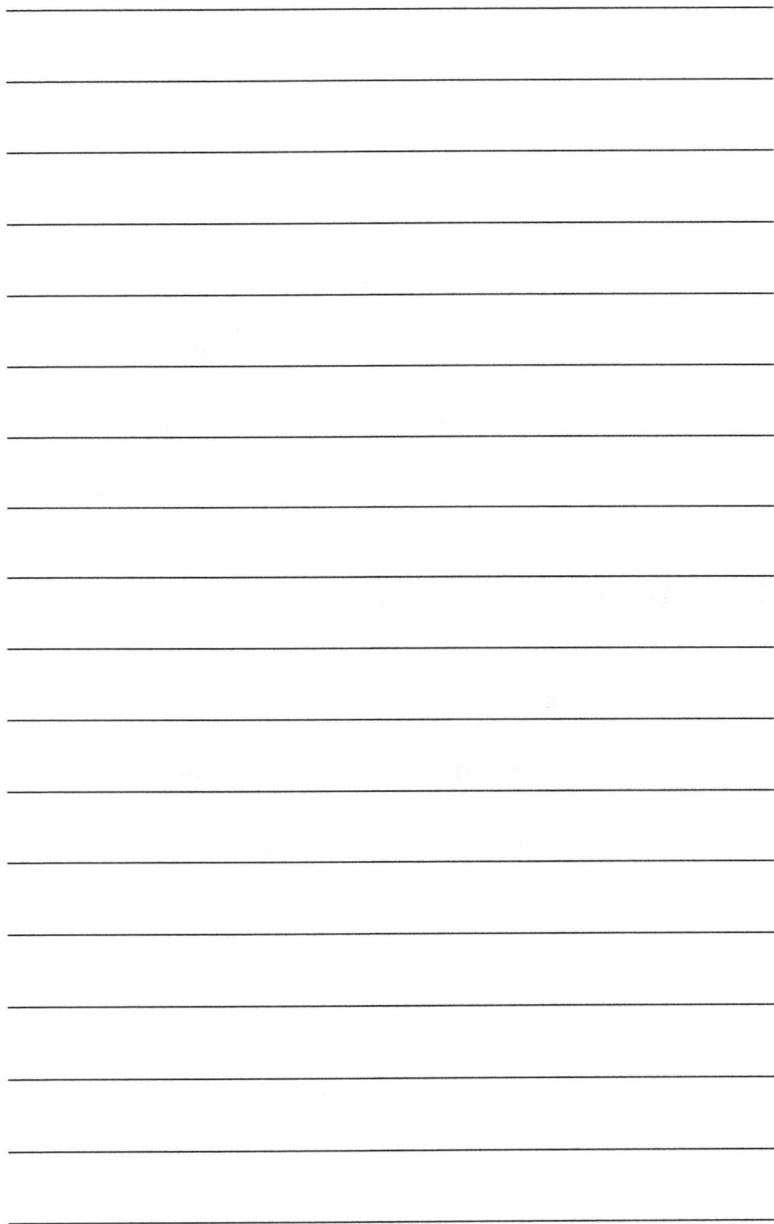

Chapter 13 The In-Between Places

We often see success stories of how a person started at the bottom, and reached the high peak of success. The middle places between the two is often glanced over. I've always had a problem with the way people speed through the process part of their success story. They race through those unsure nights, the almost places, or the I want to give it all up phases. Those places matter in the journey and there is beauty in the in-between. The in-between happens when you're not quite who you used to be, but you haven't reached your full potential either. It's the place where many people give up, and decide to retreat to their comfort zone. The in-between separates the warriors from the mediocre. The in-between is a special place I like to call "character check." Character check is the place right before elevation can take place. God must know that he can trust you with elevation. If you learn the lessons, he is sure to bring you to a new dimension. However, our fear, disobedience, and other sinful behaviors can have us continuing in a cycle like the children of Egypt in the Bible, because we won't submit our entire selves to God. We pacify ourselves with Sunday worship, and forget about him for the rest of the week. He wants to know when he blesses you, that you will use your talents to bring glory to him, and not for selfish gain. My "character check" came in the form of unemployment. I could've drowned myself in pity and blame, but I recognized my in-between place. I used my in-between wisely. I began to reflect on my previous career choices, if I was in-fact a good worker would I come in late, or do mediocre work to get through the day? I realized I always had a problem working with certain types of people. In my in-between I began intentionally working on how to work better with others, how to accept criticism, and how to behave in a work environment. My in-between wasn't punishment it was development. I had the charisma to get into the door, but I lacked the disciplined character to keep me there. It's beneficial to recognize your in-between places as moments to pause and redirect. The in-between places teach you things like humility, forgiveness, grace, positive attitudes, and work ethic. We all have areas to work on, and what better place to start. Consider the human body when it's time to grow, it becomes uncomfortable. You had to go through pain to be birthed, when your teeth had to come in, uncomfortable clothing when it was outgrown, and it's the same for you. Those uncomfortable in-between places are cause for self- evaluation, and proper action. Learn to accept the in-between place as preparation for your next assignment.

Chapter 13 Activity

Consider your in-between places. We will all be there one day as life isn't not about destinations, but about the journey. On your journey, what areas can you improve in preparation for your next phase?

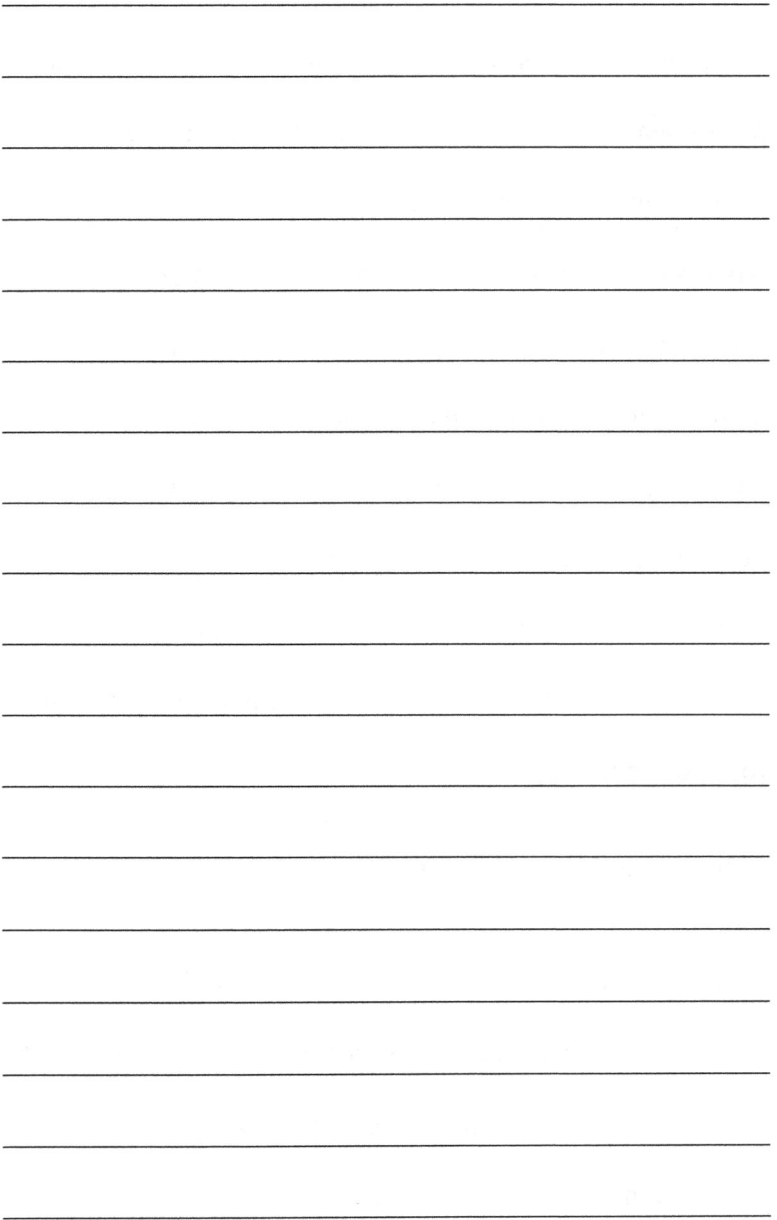

Chapter 14 Overlooked to Overbooked

In the Bible 1Samual Chapter 16, David was a shepherd boy who was overlooked and forgotten by his father and older brothers. Therefore, when Samuel was looking for the next King over Israel, it never crossed Jesse's mind to consider David as a candidate. Seven other worthy sons of Jesse had been presented to Samuel, except David. He was the youngest, smallest, and least likely to become King in the eyes of Jesse and even Samuel. God had to make Samuel send for David who was hard at work in the field. David had no rank, no wealth, and no reason to be considered for the position of king. But God had a plan for David and instead of looking at his size, his age, or his role as a shepherd boy, God looked at David's heart. Because David had a heart for God, he was appointed the second and greatest king of Israel. God raised him up from low esteem and sat him upon the throne. (1 Samuel 16:1-13) Does God have a plan for you? Has he entrusted you to do

His will and serve children? If so, he has appointed you with a great responsibility. You are valued and worthy of God's call on your life. He will not overlook you, but instead He will empower and equip you to make a difference in the lives of children. Your past has no say in the person you can become. God isn't looking for perfect Christians who have never sinned before. He wants to use those of us who survived on broken pieces. Don't broken crayons still color? How can you minister to people, and you've never been to the low places? He wants to use you, because you know what it feels like to be a sinner saved by grace. There needs to be less judgement and more love more than ever today, and you are just right for the job. Do not try to exalt yourself up, but allow God to resurrect you in time. Continue to work hard, and he will show your good deeds to the world. David did not crash the ceremony with Samuel and his father Jesse. He simply did his portion of work, and sang hymns and praises to God in his in-between time. Although there was a crowning for a King, which he was not invited to, God overlooked the popular to overbook the undervalued.

Chapter 14 Activity

Repeat and meditate on this prayer- Dear Lord Come into my life. Forgive me of the things I've thought, said, and done that is not like you. Create in me a clean heart, and renew the right spirit within me. Release from me negative thoughts that I am not worthy. Many people have counted me out, but I know you have counted me in. Form and shape me to be the person that you want me to be. Work on my thoughts, my character, my integrity, my attitude, and my body to be used by you. I am loved; I am valued; I am enough. In Jesus name, I pray Amen.

Chapter 15 Pride Comes Before Fall

My favorite scripture on pride is Proverbs 29:23 "Pride brings a person low, but the lowly in spirit gain honor." As we transition through our purpose, and God begins to elevate us, our pride can get in the way. I lost many friends and opportunities because of my prideful nature. Feelings of pride are very different from believing in one's self. For me I had pride because God elevated me over people who believed I would never make it. It felt good to rub it in their faces, and show off that I could accomplish things without their help. I was on top of the world, but slowly I began to sink again. In a world of being "self-made" it is easy to attribute one's success without considering the creator. It is God who gives us life and breath every day. He gives you the talents, strength, and tenacity to pursue your dreams. Only for you to receive the blessings and forget the creator. I had to learn not how to pray in times of trouble, but in times of blessings. When we are blessed we get lackadaisical. Our prayer life can be cut short, our worship becomes drowned out by our new schedules, and we simply don't have time to acknowledge the God that elevates us. It is important to have God be the center of all things we do. Wither it's a marriage, a business, or a career decision remembering to bring honor in everything we do will allows God to trust us with success. Proverbs 16:3 states, commit to the Lord whatever you do, and he will establish your plans. That means never get too prideful, because God is the author and finisher of our faith. If making money exceeds the will to honor God with your talents, it becomes selfish gain. At the end of your life when God asked you what you did with the talents he gave you, what will be your answer? How many people have you helped? Did you use your talent for selfish gain, or to make the world a better place?

Chapter 15 Activity

Consider what your purpose is. Is your purpose used for selfish gain or to help people? List ways your purpose can help people today?

_____

_____

_____

_____

_____

_____

_____

_____

_____

_____

_____

_____

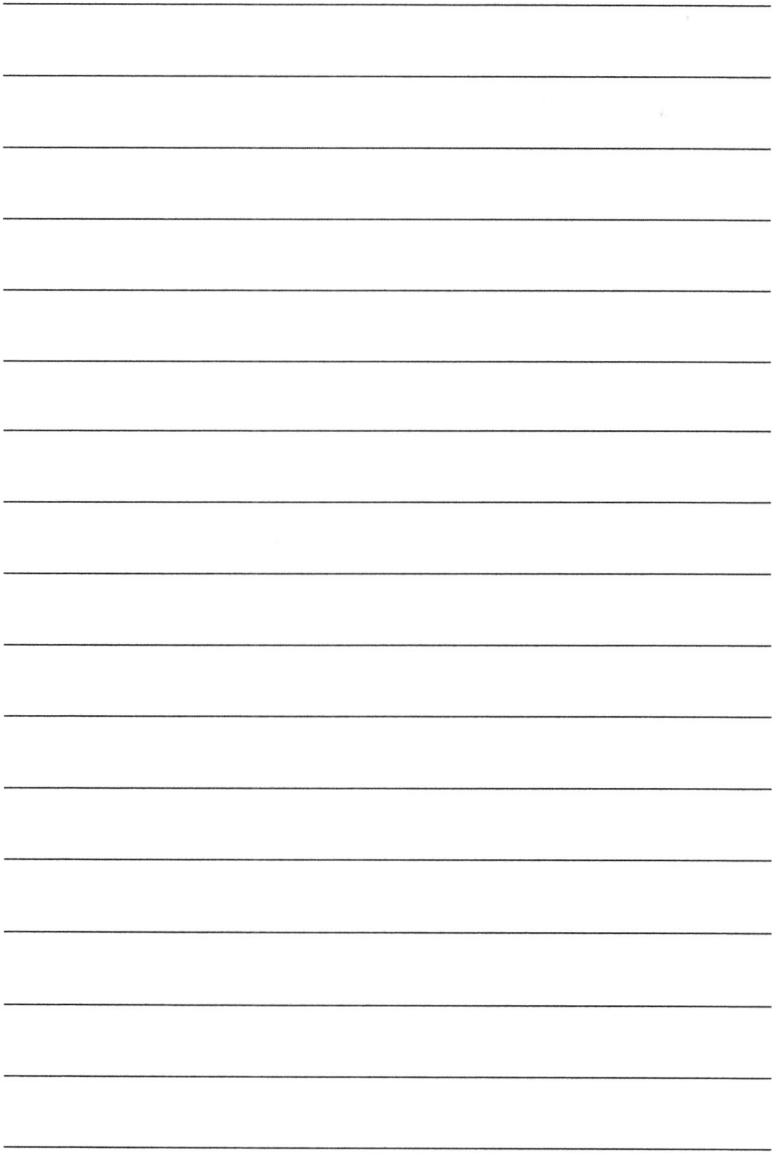

Chapter 16 Love

To understand dysfunctional relationships, I went to God, and was directed to a passage in the bible on love. We've all probably heard, and even quoted the scriptures, and still find ourselves entangled in love's nest. We sit and watch as our friends and family members find true love, and we wonder if we will ever find someone. The first step in healing from dysfunctional relationships is understanding the definition and purpose of love. 1 Corinthians 13:4-8 reads "love is patient, love is kind.It does not envy, it does not boast, it is not proud. It does not dishonor others, it is not self-seeking, it is not easily angered, it keeps no record of wrongs. Love does not delight in evil but rejoices with the truth. It always protects, always trusts, always hopes, always perseveres. Love never fails. But where there are prophecies, they will cease; where there are tongues, they will be stilled; where there is knowledge, it will pass away." Apply the scripture to your past relationships.

When we've been broken, and hurt in our youth it skews our vision of true love. We begin mimicking the love that was shown to us by our surroundings. I had to learn that love does not come to you already complete and perfect. Love may come in a package that will require work. Patience is perfected in waiting. Anything that forces you to move too quickly or does not allow you the patience to improve is not love.Dysfunctional love feels discontented, and seeks refuge outside of the commitment. Dysfunctional love is a constant feeling that your partner is going to leave you. You'll go through great lengths to sustain dysfunction like checking their phone, popping up unannounced, and even physical/ verbal abuse. Love is many things; it is not unsure. It is important to apply 1 Corinthians 13 to every relationship in our lives.

Chapter 16 Activity

Reread 1 Corinthians 13:4-8. Respond in a few sentences how you can apply the true definition of love to your current relationships, what would you do differently?

_____

_____

_____

_____

_____

_____

_____

_____

_____

_____

_____

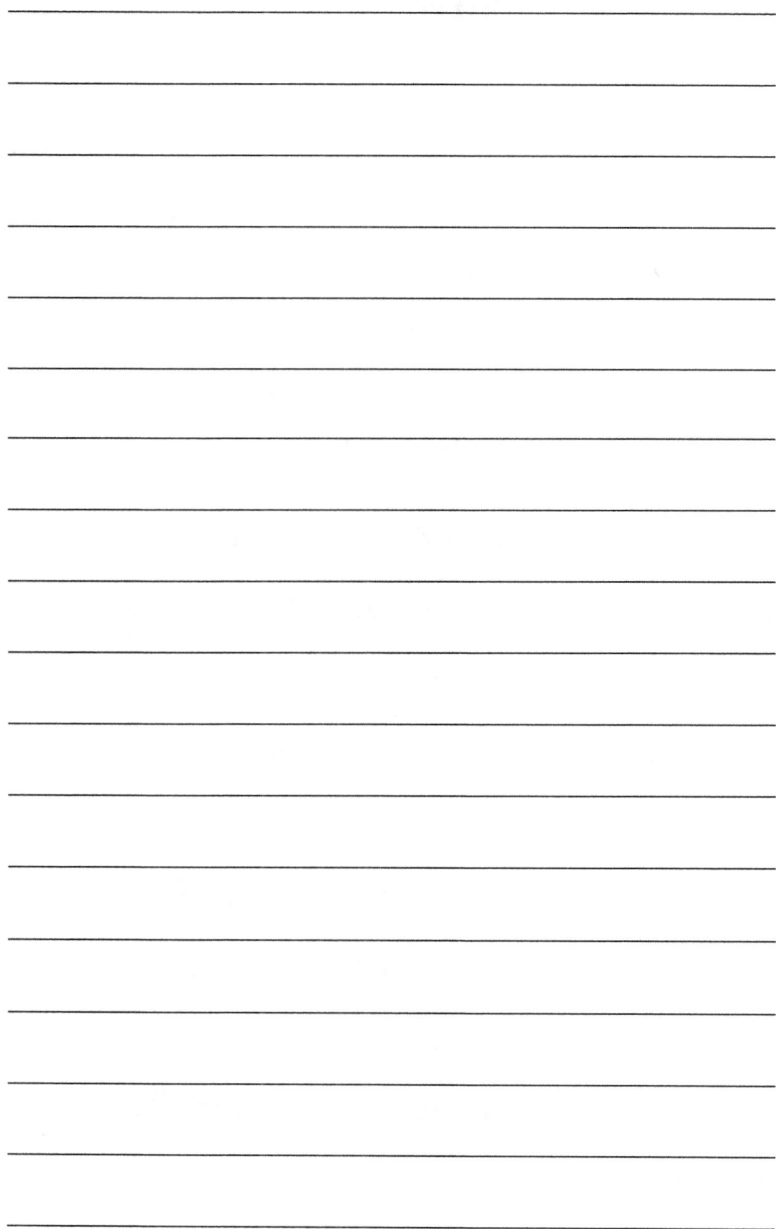

Chapter 17 Kindred Spirits

Energy is very important to sustaining functional relationships. There is a vibe we immediately pick up. It can come from body language, ulterior motives, or just a plain sixth sense. Bad energy can be felt. Have you ever noticed a slow jam song playing, and it immediately made you emotional? Have you ever listened to hardcore rap, and felt aggressive? That is a transfer of energy from one person to the next. Once I learned the meaning of love; I realized the love I was getting was far from it. I couldn't understand why I kept going in a vicious cycle of broken men, broken promises, and shattered emotions. It was then I discovered the term "kindred spirit." A kindred spirit is a person whose interests or attitudes are like one's own. Essentially all the dysfunctional people I was attracting in my life were a direct reflection of myself. The places I didn't heal, the loneliness, and isolation was a breeding ground for others who suffered with similar conditions.

Essentially any person I'd been with, my spirit was kin to in some way. It became a problem when the idea of soul ties was thrown into the mix. Soul ties are formed with every intimate relation. It is the intertwining of souls through means like sexual relations that are meant for marriage. The positive effect of a soul tie in a Godly marriage is that two become one flesh. The functionality of relationships become dysfunctional when we take matters into our own hands creating soul ties to multiple people. We pick up their habits, mannerisms, spirits, and emotional baggage as our own. Out of our loneliness we create ties with partners only meant for a season. We've intertwined our most vulnerable places with people we will never marry, with partners who don't respect or value us. We created the storm of dysfunction, and cried when it rained. The key to unlocking this toxic cycle was to end it completely. We must ask for forgiveness, and loose the ties that have bound us to certain people. If we don't completely break our soul ties, we can walk around ruining every person we try to love. We haven't healed our bodies and our hearts, and put a band aid where surgery is needed. It's vulnerable to admit we've allowed and even created the dysfunction that's present in our current relationships. But admittance is the key step in moving forward.

Chapter 17 Activity

Write a list of the names of people you may have a soul tie with due to intimate relations. Talk to God about your pain, hurt, and frustrations, and ask him to break you free from the soul-ties you have.

-
-
-
-
-
-

Chapter 18 Game Changer

Once you begin the process of functionality, you will find yourself in a place of isolation. You may physically be in group settings, but your mind is elsewhere. The place of isolation is crucial to your new positive life style change. One of my biggest misconceptions about God was that he was going to make me give up things I genuinely liked to do. Happy hours were fun, and smoking was very relaxing. Although I attended church regularly on Sunday, I wasn't giving up my fun. One Sunday morning a preacher asked the congregation, if I was to ask your social media followers or your friends, or even strangers if you represent Christ what would be their response? He went on to address how quickly we thank God for his blessings and love to receive empowering sermons, but what do we give in exchange to God? God doesn't want our lip service or Sunday drive-by. He wanted his child back, to change me, and get rid of my dysfunctional behavior. Many times, I tried it on my own account, and couldn't change. Since I gave myself to others so freely, I thought what could hurt trying it God's way? Once I gave myself over to God I felt a period of isolation. I wasn't what I used to be, but I wasn't who I wanted to be either. My conversations with my friends became strangely different. The men who realized they could no longer use me or manipulate me ran away. I was out of my comfort zone, and I didn't like it. God literally had to make people put me on the block-list, so I could focus on him. It was then I realized the place of isolation was necessary. We pray for change, but are afraid of growth. The game changed when I refused to take backwards steps. As uncomfortable, awkward, and lonely the place of isolation was, it taught me that truly functional people can stand alone. The game changed when I stopped blaming my present situations on my past. I began to take responsibility for all my actions. The game changed when I realized I was waiting on God, but he was waiting on me. He was waiting on me to choose him, to choose myself, to choose my peace and happiness, to choose purity, to choose a standard and morals for myself, to choose boundaries, to choose to be functional. I had such a hard time choosing because there were too many distractions. God literally isolated me to understand I had to lean on him for this transformation. In times of need he wanted me to call him, and not my gossiping girlfriends. He wanted me to seek him before I entered a relationship, and not when I'm broken after the whole ordeal. The place of isolation is a place of reconciliation, communication, and foundation. You can understand who your true friends are. You can clear your mind of stress and confusion. Isolation is merely separation. Your being separated from friends who aren't going in the same direction, sinful activities, harmful relationships, addictions, and anything that has tried to block your purpose. Do not fight the process embrace the stage of isolation.

Chapter 18 Activity

Meditate on this prayer of isolation today

Dear God, I thank you for allowing me to wake up today with another day to do better and to be better. I pray against the spirit of unbelief, insecurity, self-doubt, self-hatred and low self -worth. Lord show me all the wonderful things that you have created me to be able to do. Expose the lies of the enemy where these strongholds took place in my past. Help me to settle my mind and control my emotions today. Help me to understand the meaning of my isolation, and the changes I should be making now. Give me the strength to reach out and help another whenever he/she feels the compulsion to isolate and retreat from the world you want him/her to touch and heal. Thank you for the isolation for it is just separation and preparation for my destination. Amen

Chapter 19 Accountability

Accountability is the willingness to accept responsibility for one's own actions. It is a true mark of maturity on this journey to breaking dysfunctional behavior. Accountability is often uncomfortable because it means exposing your weakest areas to correction. No one wants to be publicly humiliated or made to feel bad for the poor decisions made. My greatest accountability evaluation came at the place of great pain. I had accepted a Youth Presidential term for an organization, and it was going well After time spent in the organization, I began battling with depression and extreme stress. I tried my best to conceal my depression, and continue working as the President. Our organization was having an upcoming national convention where the board and I was going to have to show what we'd been working on for the past year. I began feeling isolated from my own board members, and started keeping to myself. When the national convention came, I felt so isolated and angry with the dealings of the organization; I opted to complete my term by attending the conference, but I wasn't mentally or financially present any longer. Tensions on my board grew, and boiled over. My board called me out in front of the National President. They recited everything I ever did wrong, right in front of my face. My insides were screaming with rage. I had two options fight or flight. My flight instincts told me to cuss them out, pack my bags, and go home. I felt like I was sitting in a place where no one liked me, and no one understood what I was going through. Normalcy from my childhood experiences was to be angry from the humiliation. In the past that type of pain would've started an altercation. I instead decided that day I wasn't going to fight. I was going to listen to every negative thing said about me, and I was going to take responsibility. I made amends with my emotional and financial irresponsibility, and accepted accountability. The relationship with the organization may have been damaged, but God used that painfully humiliating experience to teach me a valuable lesson. We will not heal what we won't expose. I needed people around me who were not afraid to call me out for correction. I realized I don't have a problem with authority; I have a problem accepting responsibility for my own actions. When we become accountable in our decision making, life becomes easier. I had to get exposed publicly to heal my private battles. Don't wait until you're in front of a judgefacing time or the public to be accountable. Allow the people God has placed in your life to correct you, to be the accountability you need. Accountability partners are your parents, counselors, teachers, and elders, who are specifically placed in your life to guide you. I realized it was better to accept responsibility for my imperfection, and begin to make amends, then to continue the path of dysfunction potentially creating a worse future for myself. At any second our lives can be changed by an irrational reaction. It takes real courage to hold your peace in times of adversity. It takes strength to walk away from people who want to engage in an altercation. We will never be able to handle what people say or do to us, but that day I finally realized I have the power to control my present emotion to have a better future.

Chapter 19 Activity

Describe a point when you had to be accountable for your actions. What lesson did you learn from it? Form a list of potential accountability partners that can help guide you on this journey?

_____

_____

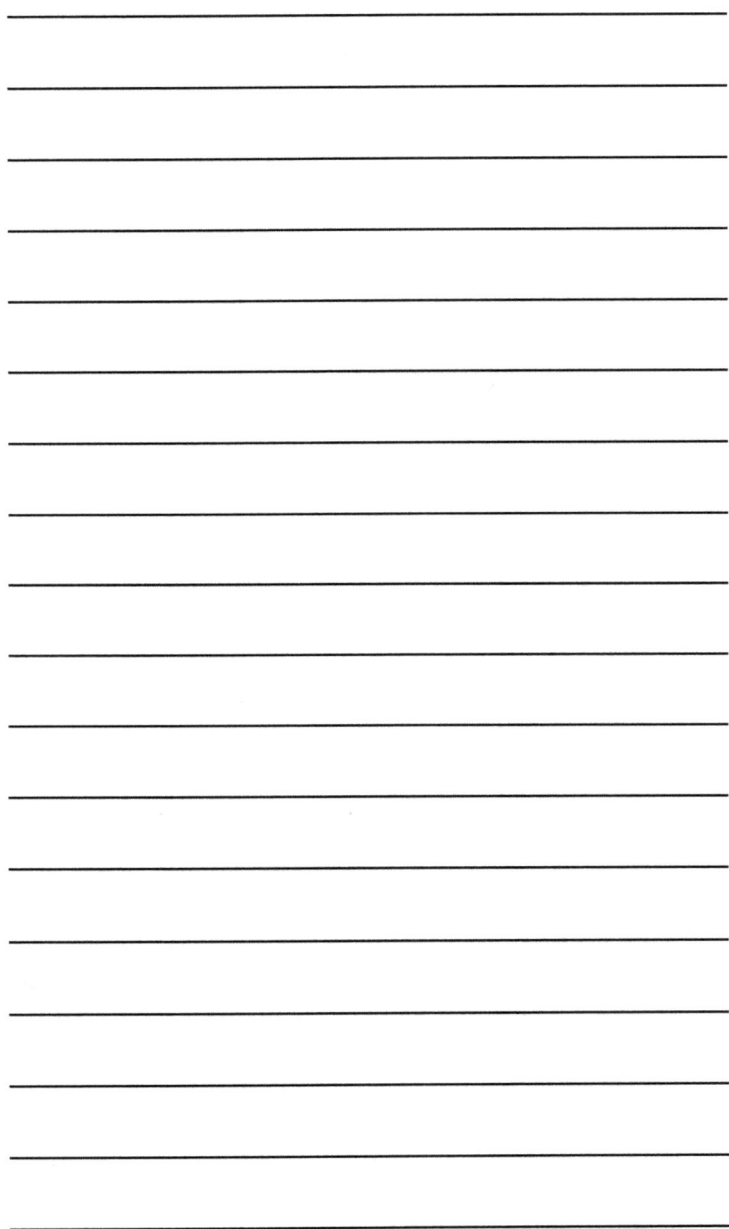

Chapter 20 Yours is the Earth and everything that's in it

As your new journey of a functional normal life begins you must learn the benefit of exposure. If you've lived in your town all your life, you're truly missing out on the world. It does not take much money or resources to expose yourself to better. Revisit the purpose chapter and the goals you wrote down. If your dream is to become a television personality, venture out of your neighborhood and find it. Research your local television stations or search the web for television internships. Unpaid internships are blessings in disguise. You discover your passion for something a lot better when you're not distracted by a paycheck. You see how bad you want it. It is the servitude and passion to learn that will set you apart from the rest. I used to believe I didn't have the money to travel and expose myself, but then I began tallying up my funds. I would spend $100-$200 at a beauty supply store buying hair that wasn't mine, from a business that did not support my community. I would spend $50 on my nails, $100 going out to eat and the club with my friends, and roughly $50 at fast food places. I totaled $400 I spent frivolously a month, which had nothing to do with the advancement of my career. Each month I sacrificed my purpose for the advancement of someone else's cream. I constantly financed other business owners, other corporations, and people who wouldn't look my way if I asked them to support my business. I began taking matters into my own hands. After I finished working my regular job I would go home and work on my craft. I began using my money for my benefit. Attending conferences and meetings concerning my purpose. I began using my money for intentional purposes only. We need to have a social life, but there was a difference between wise spending and frivolous spending I had to learn. I exposed myself to other cultures. I've lived in 7 cities before the age of 24, and I've gained a wealth of knowledge. Getting my passport was the most liberating thing I could've done. Using the excuse of not having money will only limit you. This entire world is for the taking. If you follow the guide in this workbook the earth is truly yours and everything in it. When you begin to identify your problem areas, address it, take accountability, and change it; anything is possible. Expose yourself to people in your potential work field who have been successful, expose yourself to other cultural backgrounds, music, and food. The world is much bigger than your neighborhood. It will come a time in every successful person's life when they must leave the familiar. It's better to have tried and failed and gained knowledge, then to never have tried and never know the limitless possibilities.

Chapter 20 Activities

Jot down places you want to visit and people you want to meet one day. Use your imagination and explore the possibilities. Whether the goals are small or big write a step on how you can achieve this goal

-
-
-
-
-
-
-
-
-
-

Chapter 21 The Secret

You've made it through the transformative process to breaking the dysfunctional cycle you've been in. You've learned to reach back into your childhood, and identify areas that haven't fully healed. Those unhealed areas have tarnished areas in your present life, which has brought you to this place. Functional dysfunction is a place where people continue their regularly scheduled lives either avoiding or lashing out from their unhealed places. This process has forced you to take a personal inventory. There is a purpose for your pain. There is a reason you've been through it. Everything that has happened in our lives, in some way, is linked to our future. We get clouded judgement by haters, and people who don't believe in us. We begin to believe the labels that have been placed on us. We begin to accept less than we deserve. It took me forever to realize no one needs to test drive me before marriage. My partner is perfectly capable of loving me, praying for me, covering me, and walking with me without premarital sex. It took me forever to realize I had a purpose in the field I had the most dysfunction in. My pain was preparation for my destiny. I had to identify how to be accountable for my actions, who to allow in my inner circle, and expose myself to new places. These lessons were great, but the biggest secret to my change was God. Every day I knew I was going to fail at something until I got it right. God is a never failing, never changing, consistent being. God literally saw the best in me when everyone else around me could only see the worst in me. Although it may take 21 days to change your mind, you'll spend a lifetime learning and improving. There is always going to be a new level to prepare for. No one will completely be happy every day of their lives, but with God all days are worth it. God changed my environment, my friends, and my bad habits. I constantly battled with him day in and day out, but one day I decided to honor him with my life. I decided to give him my dysfunction, and he gave me a purpose driven life. I implore you to try God this time. Try prayer in times of adversity, forgiveness in times of hurt, journaling instead of gossiping, and exposing yourself to new things and people. You are your biggest hindrance. Stop waiting for someone to save you, and save yourself today. Give up your dysfunction for a life of peace, prosperity, and purpose with God.

The End

References

Adverse Childhood Experiences Reported by Adults, 2009.
(2010). Morbidity and Mortality   Weekly   Report,
59(49), 1609-1613.

James,K.(n.d.).BibleGateway.https://www.biblegateway.co
m/versions/King-James-Version-   KJV-Bible/

Publishing
1-800-757-0598

www.ingramcontent.com/pod-product-compliance
Lightning Source LLC
Chambersburg PA
CBHW071624040426
42452CB00009B/1467